Not Everything is Black and White
An anthology of thoughts

Paul Jones

Instagram: @_paul__jones
The Fifth Chamber
Blog: https://thefifthchamberr.wordpress.com/

For Aimee and Toby
I am far greater because of you.
I love you dearly.

'Whatever you think you missed, you did'
Paul Warrior

Dear Reader,

There is no specific order in which to read these passages. They were thoughts in moments of time, inspired by conversations, images seen or events happening in the world at that point.

I hope you are able to find something specific to you in the words written. Over time with rereading and new eyes from different life experiences the value and meaning may change.

Paul

Introduction

Not content to just take part.

It can be easy to find yourself just going through the motions, getting through the work, doing the thing but not really 'doing'. Just drifting, we are all guilty of this.

Sometimes it takes someone else to see it and to say, that there is more in you, you're capable of greater. To be better.

When that happens, take it, move forward with it.

Be Purposeful with your actions.

Start

If you're thinking about starting something, you're already wasting time.

Just start.

Holdfast

But choose wisely. Everything is transient, permanence is an illusion. Nothing is given in fullness, everything needs to be fed and cultivated. Relationships, fitness, education must be continually worked on to be maintained. This is why it is important to focus on what you feed. The relationships should be two-way, they should enhance not detract from life. Those that are negative should be let go and cast aside. Education should feed knowledge, provoke questions and open the world. Fitness should expand your physical geography and reduce the restrictions of a sedentary lifestyle.

Choose well with what you hold on to.

Everything else. Let it go, do not let it burden you.

This is not a Hollywood blockbuster

This dirty grimy real life, there is no guaranteed happy ending.

However, unlike a film where you watch impotent to help.

You get to make a difference.

You can stay at home, wash your hands.

You can practice social distancing.

You can volunteer.

You can call the people in your phone book and check in.

Be kind to others and yourself.

No one person is saving the day, this is about the collective effort working together. All the little bits pulling in the same direction.

Please don't sit in the audience an static voyeur.
Move forwards, contribute.

2

Nature has claws, it's not sentimental. It is merely looking to get to the next meal, the next sunrise.

Live in the present, the now. Shedding the skin of yesterday

It is not reliant on some-one else baring the load.

It asks the question, are you capable? do you have 'claws'? Are you able to bare the load?

You should be.

Let the darkness come, fear
not the shadows. For it brings
the light into sharper focus.

Acknowledge and recognise
the negative for it is always
there and waiting. But do not
dwell upon it. Instead find the
positive, the smallest shard
and build upon it.

Fan and nurture that tiny
flame of light, feed it, make it
grow. But keep the darkness at
the edges. A timely reminder
to not become complacent.

Do not allow the flame to
extinguish

Let the fires burn bright
Do not be meek
Be bold, but with kindness
With heart and soul.
Don't be bowed or pushed down.
Hold a hand out to help others.
Be you, wonderfully you.
Laugh
Smile
Love

My Son. Just be you ♥

Inactivity is a self-imposed death sentence

Inactivity is a self-imposed death sentence.
Carried out over a prolonged period of time. It's insidious, beginning slowly, then the brake callipers slowly tighten.

The ground grows up around you. Slowly you gather dust.

Seizing up, your ability to 'do' slips away in the passing of time. Until 'can' becomes 'can't'. The phrase 'when I was younger' becomes the currency of excuses.

There is the possibility of release from the death sentence. It is available, right at the edge of your consciousness. The tingle in the finger tips from the promise of movement.

It starts with one step, followed by another. It's likely to be a long path to be free of the bonds of inactivity. But it's a path a growth.

It opens up the map.

Take the step. It does not need to be grand.

Perpetual.

Beautiful and deadly in equal measure.

Never the same from one moment to the next.

reflection
/rɪˈflɛkʃ(ə)n/

Serious thought or
consideration.

Use the time to look back on
your experiences. Good, bad,
happy and painful. They all
offer a lesson and an opportunity
to move forwards and develop
further. The lessons aren't always
immediately obvious, it is often
only with time that the message/
learning reveals itself.

The reality is that all experiences leave their mark on us
whether physical, mental or
emotional. Each burns deeper
than we realise.

We are guests on this
wonderful sphere. In time
we will return to it, to the
earth, a fact of life.

Cherish it
It's power
It's grace
The sharp edges
The smooth lines
It's the only one we have.

9

perspective
/pəˈspɛktɪv/

a particular attitude towards or way
of regarding something; a point of
view.

How you choose to respond to a
situation is down to you. It is not
pre-ordained but it does take effort.

You can choose to take the best
out of each situation and move
forward.

Or

See nothing but negatives and be
trapped in a downward spiral.

It's up to you.

The tide never stops

Often the end of the year is a time of reflection, looking back on what has been.

Cherishing the precious moments that have past.

Acknowledging challenges that have been encountered.

Touching the hand that got burnt and embracing lessons learnt.

But remember the tides never stop, always moving forward.

So as we move into 2020. Keep moving forward. Be it one step at a time or a giant leap. Just keep moving, be the your own tide.

Happy New year.

The tide returns, relentless in its movement.

There is no emotion just the constant ebb and flow.

Mirroring life and death.

You don't need to hold on to all the stones on the beach. Keep the important ones and let the tide wash over the rest.

Do not be weighed down by the rest.

growth
/grəʊθ/

Feed and nourish ideas, performance,
relationships. Enjoy the patience required for
them to come to fruition.

Neglect them and they will wilt and perish.

Fluctuation / ˌflʌktʃʊˈeɪʃ(ə)n, ˌflʌktjʊˈeɪʃ(ə)n/

noun: fluctuation; plural noun: fluctuations an irregular rising and falling in number or amount; a variation.

The rhythm of life is not linear. There is a constant ebb and flow. Be it perceived success or failure, highs and lows. I think the lesson is not to fight against these, but to acknowledge them, understand that they happen.

Then learn to navigate through those periods and use them to develop and move forward.

Harvest. /ˈhɑːvɪst/

the process or period of gathering in crops.

You can't just plant the seed you need to
nurture it, feed and tend to it.

It is the same for all things that you wish to
grow. You cannot neglect it, for it will wilt and
fade away.

Keep feeding your goals with good energy, you
wouldn't put weed killer on your veg, so leave
the negative thoughts.

Carrots from the garden.

Do not allow your environment to be an excuse.

It starts and ends with you. All that you need you already have but you need to search for it. It won't just appear.

Try
Try again
Ask questions
Fail - learn
Try again.

Don't expect it to just happen. It won't.

When the storm comes

Tears – Tiers
Fears – Fear

You can hear the fear on the patients voice. The same fear that is etched on the owner of a business barely holding on.

Is there a difference in the bitter taste of that fear?

I think not.

So many talk in absolutes even when there are still so many unknowns.

When the storm comes we hold on tight and navigate as best we can not knowing the safest path. Only learning the full cost when we reach calmer waters.

We are still holding on, seeking a path. Do not lose your grip. Do not lose your head.

Conversation

The conversation can often be the unrealised start, the catalyst to an idea.

A two-way street of dialogue, experience sharing. Where what you say is important but what you hear is crucial.

The point is not to listen to answer. But to listen to hear.

To understand what has been said. To feel, to take on board.
To appreciate intimacy from the sharing of experience.

Do not be quick to reply, give time to what has been said, what has been offered. Let it settle and absorb. Allow the words to play out. Too often we reply without thought or understanding.

Return to the conversation, give the words space and develop it further. The silence is a powerful tool.

Flexibility and openness, prerequisites to taking it further. Avoiding the destination being a dead end.

Courage in challenging long held believes, offering a key to opening a locked door.

The gold is rarely found in the first sifting of the sieve. Do not settle for fool's gold.

The lost opportunities of life are found in the face of death

Perhaps the true value of life is only fully appreciated in the shadows of death.

It changes, abruptly, the lens that is used to observe the world. Shining light on missed experiences, opportunities not taken, words left unspoken.

It is suggested that life flashes before the eyes in the face of death. Yet many find themselves negotiating "if I get through this I will do the thing…". Yet to often after survival those words fade into a hollow void, lost and forgotten in the comfort blanket of routine and a return to 'normal life'.

There are those, that take hold of the sharp cold edges of the that lens that

death provides. The viewpoint of life shifted, seeing the world with different eyes. Understanding that time ticks on indefinitely unlike the unguaranteed beating of a heart.

This, this is the time when death becomes a gift and life is no longer taken for granted.

The paradigm shift.

It is not easy, often painful and potentially lonely – the raising of ideas and thoughts that have long been pushed under the surface. Hidden in the subconscious, to afraid to be admitted too and act upon.

Maybe this is why death is so painful, not just for the loss of a loved one but the mourning of the lives that live on being unlived and unfilled.

Perhaps this is the greatest sadness in death.

The missed opportunities.

Do not wait.

Time continues.

The shadow man and the watching ghosts

I am a shadow of the man I am yet to become, while the ghosts of whom I have been watch at the edges.

There are successes and failures, high and lows. Moments of pride and regret. They need to be remembered so that the lessons learned can be taken forward. But they do not need to be carried, repeatedly revisiting them leads to walking backwards and getting a stiff neck.

The lessons help to increase the successes the moments of pride and reduce the regrets moving forwards.

Kaizen a Japanese word meaning continuous improvement, gradual and methodical. A slow moving constant change for the better.

Perhaps this is the best path to moving forward, from the shadows, let the ghosts gather and watch from the edges.

Be restless in the progress enjoy what happens and what has been and humble towards what has gone before.

For we are never truly the finished article. Push forward.

Poisoned sweetness of the group consensus. Independent thought is the currency of knowledge.

It has been said that the world not as it is but as we are. It is seen from our own viewpoint, our own colouring and shading.
Based on the experiences allied to the beliefs of those close to us.

Often being pulled along, taking things on face value and riding the current of a populist view.

But there is danger in riding the current as a passive passenger – you have no control where you are going.

The rudder is to be found in the ability to question and critically appraise. That is not to say the populist view is always wrong or right, the trap is in believing the first to shout or the ones with the loudest voice. Often passing off their believe as fact.

The same can be said when working in a group with all agreeing to what seems an obvious answer or way. The statement 'we do it this way because that's how we've always done it'.

There is danger in consensus without question or critique.

A narrowing of vision stuck with our own blinkers, unable to reposition ourselves and look at the world or situation from another's experience, another's pair of eyes. To often afraid that, just maybe we are wrong, that a different way could be better. Or worse still the foundation of our believes is made of sand, or is waiting to tumble like a wobbling Jenga tower.

Add a critical lens, don't be afraid to question. Scratch the surface, grab a shovel and dig a little deeper.

Independent thought is high currency in the accumulation of knowledge. Avoid lazy consensus and conformity.

Adapt or Decay

2020 has potentially given more opportunity to learn, develop and grow than any other year.

Just as, not everything that glitters is gold, equally not all gold glitters. Sometimes it is wrapped in barbed wire or covered in faeces. Many will look away unable to see the value of what is presented. Unable to see the landscape, short-sighted, blinded. Maybe myopia is the unseen pandemic.

It has been a challenge that very few have ever encountered before. And yet, take the time to think clearly, uncluttered with previous restrictions and maybe just maybe good things can happen. The forced adaptation, creating rapid change where necessity gives birth to invention.

In high-stakes situations/performance/sports, often 'it' just needs to get done, a workable solution

within the boundaries, you find a way. Life is pretty high-stakes These moments are uncomfortable, often painful and comes with an emotional cost but it is worth the exchange.

Adversity will often reveal the true character of an individual, not always the carefully curated social media imagine. More tarnished, scraped and rough edged. There has been time to reflect, understand what is important and what is not. The non-negotiables to be held tight and stay central to all that you do. Whilst allowing you to jettison that, that is not important, the fluff and the noise, drown it out.

Do not allow the noise to resurface, weigh it down with concrete boots.

The reality is nothing stays the same, evolution continues unchecked but perhaps these times allow for strides to be made and not a two-step shuffle with laces tide together.

Make sure the knife is sharp, cut the tether. Firm hands to grab the barbwire and wash the shit off the gold with fresh clear thoughts.

Adapt or decay.

The unknown and unseen emotional transaction in human exchange

The interaction between two people has an unseen and unknown emotional transaction.

It's an unknown that we readily accept even chase, multiple times a day. Without a true understanding of the consequences, we have a 'hoped for' outcome but it is never guaranteed. Believing that it stops at the end of the interaction, it rarely does.

Often there is a brief interaction with a small short lived echo from a 'good morning, you okay?' or a brief annoyance of someone not using their car indicator at a junction. That sits briefly but is not lasting.

Then there are the lasting interactions, where the exchange is greater, an emotional transaction, the ones that 24hrs, a week later and beyond cause an onward ripple.

The transaction can often be one-sided and unknown to donor/recipient.

It can go both ways, it can bring a lightness and joy and leave the individual feeling like they are on cloud nine and give them the launchpad to greater things. Conversely it can leave the recipient heavy, carrying an emotional burden, or leave them empty.

Perhaps the highest cost is found in those who provide a close service or high emotion, where the recipient has a emotional investment. Parents to a child, close friends' teachers, coaches, mentors and clinicians to mention a few. Where the support is given readily, energy and emotion the currency, draining the givers cup. Multiply that by the number of transactions each day, each week and the cup drains quickly.

It is a silent, invisible transaction, lost on half of the participants. For it is an individual experience, with the full cost not immediately apparent. Yet at the end of the day the needle is firmly bending towards the E for empty.

It is more than just the words spoken, the expression and the intonation. It's the accompanying body language setting the tone, and shifting with the flow of the conversation, underlining and emphasising what is being said.

But perhaps it's the one on one eye contact when the words are said that carries more weight than the words themselves. They show the true meaning, the true value of the exchange.

Ultimately the cost is relative to the individual and their ability to be open and reflective. The interactions offer so much.

They teach us.
Shape us.

They are privileged moments.

Missed by too many. Be mindful of what you give and what you take.

Make sure your ceiling has an escape hatch

Too often we stop.
We put the handbrake on.
We stop developing, improving, refining our craft. Mentally we drop anchor, believing that this is as far as we can come. Proud of the distance we have travelled, self congratulatory believing that we would never reach this point. Making it okay to rest and settle, our head touching the ceiling of self imposed capability.

Maybe something has happened, a significant life event that has helped to cast the anchor off. But then life is not linear.

There is great power in the ability to 'try again', to explore the previously unsuccessful attempt and learn the lesson and apply the teaching. Then try again.

Sometimes that is from within the individual, that stubbornness that drives them. Other times it comes from an external voice, a nudge of encouragement, pointing the finger to a different approach. It can be a comforting arm that says it's okay to not succeed the first, third or ninth time but seeing gradual improvement. However, persistence is required. Then there is the firm direct voice that welds a stick because that is what is required.

Very rarely do we reach our true ceiling. Yes there will be limiting factors, priority, understanding, knowledge, opportunity, time. Many of these are pliable, they can be change but effort is required.

Few, if any are flawless. There is always room for improvement.

You're not 'there' yet, keep going. Take pleasure in the effort, the work. Embrace the challenge. By all means look back and see the ground you have covered, use that as a foundation for the future, not as a monument to the past.

When you hit the ceiling, open the hatch. If there is no hatch, make one. As for help if needed. Breakthrough.

When you burn the shed skin, discover who you are

Identity and self are curious things, frequently they are inappropriately used interchangeably.

The power to shape and change both sits in the individuals hands. Yet too often we do neither and allow others to assign identities or rely on what we do to become our identity/label without ever truly knowing our self.

Your identity, knowing yourself and showing your true self are very different, overlapping each other. We inevitably show multiple versions of ourselves depending on the situation. At work, our parents, new people and the self you share with your closest friends/loved ones. Then there is the social media version, to often the highlights, the projection of who we want people to think we are. Brief 2 dimensional Polaroids.

The identity that people know you by will inevitably be different to the identity that you relate to. Often the difference is small, the subtle choice and style of language differentiating the two. The level of information shared or more importantly the information not shared. Sometimes it is not the words but the actions of the individual that shows their true self.

Throughout our lives the versions of ourselves should change as experience and exposure shapes us. We refine our identity and self, burning the shed skin, the old parts as we move forward. To stay stuck, fixed throughout your life would be a betrayal and waste of those moments both bitter and sweet.

The key, and this is the hard part, is to learn to know your true self and hold on to your core values. This is what takes time, requiring reflection, honesty and insight. You won't like everything, nor should you for that is unrealistic. There is also a level of bravery needed, to standfast, not to go in the opposite direction just because others what you to go there.

Be bold, explore and discover your own 'self', be true to it. Do not waver, for the self belongs to no other but you.

Burn the shed skin.

I do not know everything

To acknowledge that you are not perfect, that you do not know everything is extremely powerful. It allows for the opportunity to move forward, to be better. Understand that you do not know everything, to suggest otherwise would arrogant and foolhardy.

To proffer oneself as an expert is perhaps, at best a display of ego, flexing and showing off like a peacock displaying it's feathers. At worst, pure vanity and pride full of hubris, oozing disdain for those who you ordain to be below you.

However, recognition of expertise, of being an expert by you peers is quite another thing. It should, perhaps come with a caveat of being humble, open to others, approachable. To be arrogant and closed cancels out the knowledge that you might share.

The best teachers are those that learn from their students, that allow the opportunity for a different perspective. That see an opportunity for learning to be a two-way street. Happy to have a blank page in a never ending book ready to be filled with more.

Formal study it is often driven by attaining the qualification, the piece of paper. That is not to discredit or underplay the value or work put in as that opens the door. But maybe, in retrospect we notice it is more about climbing up upon the first step, preparing you for the 'true' lessons that you gather through experience and consolidation.

The learning that is driven by the internal desire to know more about a subject, to be better at an activity. Often has greater gravity, it hold more because it is personal.

The learning gives way to more and more questions. It takes us further.

Learn like a novice devouring information but with the patience of grand master. There is always more to learn, someone to learn from. Never be to proud to say I don't know. The only silly questions are the ones you don't ask.

Read between the lines

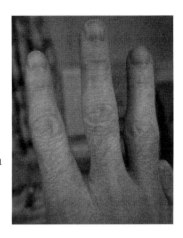

Read between the lines.
Not everything you see is all that is being shown.
Don't be taken in by the bright shiny lights and the loudest shouts.
The agenda behind the sensory bombardment is rarely beneficent.

Disagree and be angry but by saying something is wrong and not providing an alternative is just adding more noise. Just noise does not move the conversation or situation forward. It more likely digs the heals in and becomes more difficult to move, more rigid and more divisive.

What is the viable alternative, offer that and people listen, discuss. Then the shape and route forwards changes.

It's easy to tear down, to destroy and criticise anyone can do it. To suggest, to build, to create, to be courageous. That takes something else, something more.

Focus your energy on that and maybe things start to get brighter.

But don't be fooled into thinking everyone will like what you suggest and do all of the time.

That's a fairytale, with rarely a happily forever after.

The thorns matter

The sharp painful, inhospitable parts are interwoven with the beautiful.
They are part of the whole.
They hold a beauty in their own right, perfectly formed, developed and
evolved over time to fulfil a specific purpose.

The sharp hard parts of life are there for a reason. Not always immediately obvious.
They shape, mould and develop us.
We are not meant to stay the same, we endure, weather the storm, to then
bask in the sun again.

Lessons taken and strategies created.
The needle pushed forward, the baseline refreshed.

Nothing is given by right. It is earned through adaptation, perseverance,
relentless will.
The thorns allow the growth, fight off the opposition, so that the rose can bloom.

The thorns matter.

And if all else fails. You can pluck them from the stem stick it to your nose and pretend to be a rhino.

Walk with Curiosity

To start is the tricky bit, that first step, but inertia holdsfast.
Procrastination sets in.
Should I do it like this person or maybe like that one over there.
Too often overthinking and making unhelpful comparisons.

And yet.
As babies we make that first step.
We start walking without comparison or concern. The path of movement and exploration started.
Walking step by step repeating the process, developing the gait, our own style.

The result? A steady expansion of the physical world. Eyes wide. Drinking in all it has to offer.
Senses alive to all.
Colours
Smell
Texture
Sounds and more.
Experiencing the wonder of everything a new.

The age increases and the wonderment fades, the experience of discovery in too many reduced, lost in a dusty corner. Forgotten.

The feet become stuck as is fastened by roots, burdened by an unseen load.
Struggling to begin, to take the step into the next physical and metaphorical expedition.
Unable to break new ground, creating barriers and finding excuses.
Instead preferring to follow the crowd, the herd. Like cattle.
Taking the well trodden, popular, fashionable, unencumbered route.

The chances are we have all be guilty of this, maybe only briefly.
Hanging on to the coattails of others.
Being led by a guide, pulled along, sheltered.
Guides can be great, they will show you many things, highlights, things know to them, liked by them.
Maybe even helping you to get to a certain point.

However, what they show you is not necessarily what you need to see or experience.
The learning, the true exploration begins when you let go of the hand. Beginning to travel by your own compass.
Not mollycoddled.
Exposed to the four winds.

Often seeming to suffer and struggle, making mistakes. Burning our hands.
Only to realise that we were becoming more than before.

There will be times when we cross paths with others.
Briefly in the same space.
Understanding that the steps taken, the experiences gathered to get here completely different.

The intersection providing a crucible of ideas, understanding
of the experiences gained and teachings learned.

A pause
Reflection

Before re orientating and moving onwards.

Lean forward, you'll either fall on your face or take the
first step.

Either way it will be what you need. Waking you up or
moving forward.

Do not underestimate the bare tree

Shed of its leaves.
Discarding that, that is of no use.
Optimising it energy.
Sentient.
Watching over the landscape
It stands firm, roots gripping the earth, yet flexible to the bending winds.

Understanding the unforgiving cycle of nature.
Just as there are days when the tree is in full leaf, basking in the sun, drinking from deep roots.
So to there are days of harsh winds and battering storms.

Quietly it's moving, the buds of growth are starting to shoot. Its pushing it's roots deeper making its
base stronger.

Just as the tree does these things so should we.
Remove all that does not share a purpose in the goals that have been set.

Deepen and widen our base to make
secure our position.
Flexible enough to bend and move
around the harsh realities of life
without breaking.
Preparing and building our energy.
To build upon the foundations.

There is much more to be taken
from the tree than just a place to lean
against.

Just watch for dogs peeing against
your legs.

41

There is pleasure in being up early in the dark

Before the world wakes.
The early morning darkness cool and clear, has a calm and comforting quality.
There is a stillness not found once the world is awake and the sky lit.

The shadows long, the dark making the world seem smaller.
The silent motionless of a day yet to start, holding you accountable for all your movements.

To make too much noise and it is a like a spotlight shinning on you.
Be respectful of the hour and you get to stay in the shadows. The work unseen, closed eyes staying shut.

As sense of achievement, the work done has an honest quality. Not done to entertain or impress.

There is comfort and a sense of attachment to the world around you found in the bird song in the background.
Heard between the soundtrack of breathing and internal dialogue.

The peace and rising light bringing a clear head after the effort given.

Embrace the dark, the calm, breath it in. Take it forward.

Consequence

There is always a consequence to action or inaction.
Intended or not.
To suggest otherwise or try to apportion blame to another is at best, both lazy and naive.

Ownership is required, mandated. You are not inanimate.
Sometimes the consequence is immediate, touching a hot dish and burning you.
The feedback instant, the learning taught.

Other times it gradually evolves the consequence not obvious initially.
There are subtle changes.
Not initially discernible but slowly coming to light.
These can carry great weight both positive and negative.
Moving, unseen yet important pieces on the chessboard, positioning them, waiting for checkmate.

Understanding consequence or the potential for consequence as part of an equation;
Intention +/- action = consequence.
Perhaps allows the individual to start to effect the continuum. Understanding why it happens then grasping that YOU can affect it, can become a superpower.

Intention – purpose, wish, desire, to stretch out, go further.

Yet Intention is too often the opening words of a lost opportunity, remaining as lines on a page or throwaway words, failing to materialise into action.

'It was my intention to do….' passive and hollow, they remain marked on paper or a distant echo, a reminder of inaction.

We frequently fail to do the 'thing' yet wonder why it didn't happen, a hoped for consequence not realised.

Still we continue to hope for, to want it and do nothing to move closer.

Only when we change the dialogue, the sentence to "I did this" can the first step that leads to the end result, be claimed. Dropping the 'intent – ion" and swapping it for intent "I did this with intent today" starts to shift the paradigm.

Frequently, with big change, it is rarely a singular endeavour, but the first step has to be taken by the individual. Endurance is needed, worthwhile change is rarely immediate.

Despite wanting the 'it' to be now, to happen instantaneously, patience becomes an unlikely yet needed bedfellow.

It sits like a heavy yoke, weighing you down, wanting to shrug it off, to forget it.

When it becomes too heavy what starts the process is important to remember, to refer back to. Make it a book that you read often to remind yourself why.

If it all seems too big just read a line or one word that keeps the intent from becoming intention. Remain active avoid becoming passive and inert.

Accepting ownership is crucial. Not just of your actions but your response to others.
Both are of equal importance.
Being 'triggered' ultimately is a choice, the response, your action or inaction the emotional retaliation is in your hands.

This not a case of compromising principles. Instead it is a case of choosing to invest your energy towards that, that is ultimately important and drives towards the goals. Not being derailed.

The responsibility sits with the individual. There will always be external forces pushing and pulling. But it will always start and end with the self.

Consequence is important and unavoidable but yours to shape.

Do not forget this.

Power – Energy

Who or what holds yours?
Who holds the switch, the supply, the source?

Your, our, energy is precious.
But we allow it to bleed out without even realising it.
Leaving the small cuts open, ignoring them and not applying
pressure.
Inviting leeches covered in glitter to take, to drink deep,
empty and leave us void.

Too easily we stand by the drain, letting it siphon away all
that we give conscious or otherwise.
We keep close the toxic relationships, held to them on cast
away platitudes, hoping for the best, yet never receiving it.

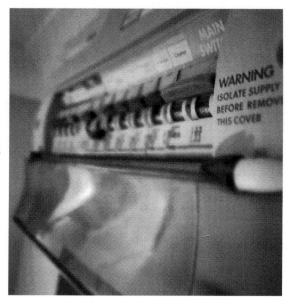

The blue light holding like a tractor beam, poisoned honey dripping through the USB port or into our
ears. Holding on to the gadgets that use us like a battery.

Preferring the sugar coated, bright lights of the blue pill, when the bitter red pill should be grasped. The
echo of childhood, where your told the best medicine tastes horrible.

Those that we keep close should be considered and cultivated.
Cut and weed the parasites out, burn the roots.
Instead look for symbiosis. The sharing of good energy.
Sadly it is not colour coded so thought and reflection is needed. Due diligence must be paid.

Be aware of not only those that drain you but also feed. Bad energy will perpetuates and infect. Rot spreading through ultimately bringing desolation.

Wire clippers work well to cut the draining cables.

Find those with similar energy heading the same way. There should be differences but the tenor remains. The sharing, good energy begets good energy. Like streams converging into a torrent, a great river.

You are not bound by contract. You choose, sometimes the choice is wrong. Don't dwell, just remove, no more energy needs to go there. Isolate the supply. You control the fuse box, the switches. Sit in the dark for a while, get comfortable for you will realise you don't need all that you've been plugged into.

The reality is the power is yours, when you understand this. Only then will you see the glimmer of light.

Scars

Scars are often the unknown first line or the first word of the challenge to come and the subsequent lesson to be learned. The physical is obvious, surface level for all to see. It is the emotional and psychological scars that are deeper, unseen with greater roots and far reaching echos over time.

The physical scar is the entry point to dealing with pain and often the removal of 'normal'. They teach us to adapt, to overcome. They walk hand in hand with struggle, the ability to endure, presenting unrequested but perhaps, needed lessons in endurance and fortitude.

Often behind the physical is the emotional and psychological it is the beginning of a

long road, with anger, frustration, sadness, regret, opportunity and pain as companions on a pot holed road. They are yours to carry, to stare down and cast off.

The physical scar more often than not, whilst remaining visible, is short lived a brief painful inconvenience. Protocol's written to help guide the recovery, sometimes there will be a lasting change but more often a return to what was occurs. They are outwardly visible for all to see and share and sympathise. They do not leave us, marked indelibly for good, they may fade but a legacy is left. At best a cool story at worst a lasting insurmountable hurdle.

It is the mental and emotional scars that linger, often becoming bigger and deeper as time passes. They grow in the dark recesses of the mind becoming barriers to opportunities, self-created monsters, vessels of fear and self-doubt. But they are not set in stone, they can be tamed and sunk, recovery and rehabilitation are not false hopes. There will be time needed sitting with the self, some internal exploration of what has happened, reflection and understanding that the past cannot be changed but the future can be shaped. You need to choose to actively carve that shape, that future. Lead with an empty open hand, outstretched to ask for help for rarely is the rehabilitation completed unaccompanied.

It is important to note that: The recovered self is never the same as the one prior to the insult. Too much has come to pass, time, energy, emotion and then something deeper.

For me, I physically have a lengthy longitudinal scar on each knee but the cuts went a lot deeper. For me one scar represents a stolen identity, a forfeited future, a path into a dark place that took 10 years to head back to the surface. When the second one happened it grabbed me by the neck and pulled me through the surface the darkness and malaise dissipating, allowing a variety of tones to flood through.

The reality is both are equally as valuable as the other. They have given far more than they have taken though it has perhaps with the passing of time acknowledgement of this has come. I would not swap the scars they are indelible reminders of life lived, endeavour, overextension and the road back. Like rings on a tree, they are marks in time. A commentary on experience, to run your finger along the length is to read a line in history like the groove of classic vinyl.

Maybe the reality is we are constantly undergoing rehabilitation, physical, mental and emotional, dancing along the spectrum of 'self', with all outcomes infinite and undetermined.

SELF

Accept who you have been Acknowledge who are now Be excited for who you can become.

The future is not set in stone, do not get stuck in the trap of believing it is already written.

Take a look in the mirror, decide where you want to go and start actioning it.

Don't be passive.
Don't be done to.
I am becoming.
You are becoming.

Environment: Flourish or Fester?

Too often we lose focus on our immediate surroundings. To busy looking further afield or at the screen 12 inches away from our nose.

We forget the importance of our environment, the impact it has on us and us on it. The environment is not just confined to the physical objects, the bricks and mortar, trees and grass. But the people that feed into it. Either face to face or through a screen. The energy we consume.

The environment can elevate you, feed you, see you develop, grow and flourish. It will pull you along and upwards, put and arm around you and protect you. Or give a kick in the shin's when you need a timely reminder to let go of the things you have no control over.

The environment can have a dark and malevolent side. It can rob you of your growth, make you stagnate as if pot bound and keep you down. It can poison insidiously, creeping unnoticed, dragging you under and starving you of nutrients and life. Sapping your energy and taking your enthusiasm.

The environment can be harsh and unforgiving and yet it will teach you. It can be glorious and beautiful and take your breath away.

Whilst you cannot control everything, there is the power of choice. You can construct and cultivate that, that surrounds you. What you accept to consume.

The environment should enrich, develop and help you to move forward. Be supportive, bring joy and love whilst challenging you to be better.

Stop and take a look at your environment, does help you grow or is slowly contaminating and poisoning you. Then check the mirror and make sure your not the contaminant.

Sometimes you need to change the soil, dig deep and sow new seeds. Other times you just need to do the weeding.

53

The Tie and the Noose are not so different

Fear, anxiety and self-doubt all sit like a noose around the neck, it weighs heavy tightening to the point just prior to suffocation. It sits waiting to be pulled tighter, dressed as anxiety. Like a lead in the hands of an over enthusiastic handler.

Its painted it to look like fancy tie and worn with false confidence, an adornment to a suit of fragility. It may change how it looks but the weight remains. Heavy.

Both are carried, always pulling down against gravity, yet the wearer has learned to make it look like a ring of feathers, light and almost invisible. Except sometimes the smoke and mirrors are not there and it like Atlas, the weight of the world sits upon them without the Titan's strength.

Relief can sometimes be found in distraction all be it brief before the hangman pulls sharp and hard and the relief evaporates. Look into the hangman's face and all you see is your own.

The noose of self-doubt grows ever tighter in the darkness. The darkness created by silence and inward self discussion. Not until the voice turns outward and begins to share can the narrative begin to change. A slight loosening, a normal breath. The downward screw changing direction. Now you can grasp the sharp shard of light, you can start to cut and tear open the frayed edges of the noose.

But know, just as your shadow remains even in the dark. The hangman and his noose are always close. Do not fall silent, keep talking for your voice helps to keep him at arm's reach.

Shhh
Can you hear that?

That's the power of Your voice.

55

Carve a line

If you don't like where you are, who your with or what you are doing.

It's time to carve a line, carved deep so as not to be erased, move forward from it and create change.

Too often the 'can't' or 'excuse' is self created and then perpetuated internally. Guilty of thinking it needs to be big dramatic change. Instead start with small changes and accumulate them.

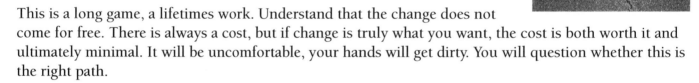

This is a long game, a lifetimes work. Understand that the change does not come for free. There is always a cost, but if change is truly what you want, the cost is both worth it and ultimately minimal. It will be uncomfortable, your hands will get dirty. You will question whether this is the right path.

This is normal.

Over time the eyes in the mirror will not look the same, they will change. They should tell an unspoken story of the distance traveled beyond the carved line. This is not a passenger ride. You have to take the wheel. Ask for help, for directions but you must drive it.

Carve your line – move forward.

The Echo chamber is a dead end

We are told that we are the sum of the five people closest to us. That we should surround ourselves with like-minded people. People that will build us up and push us forwards. To cut away the detractors, those that have opposite values or hold us back.

We should curate who we hold close or allow ourselves to be influenced by. Whether in person or the media. However, whilst this can be both true and beneficial it can have pitfalls. Curate by all means but be careful not to isolate and/or discriminate.

The risk is that we dive into a self-perpetuating echo chamber. Running on a treadmill of rumination and cherry-picked rabbit holes. We should be exposed to opposite ideas, different ways of doing things. Ignorance should not be an excuse.

The challenge comes not from conflicting ideas or different ways of doing something. The true challenge is in our ability to critically analyse the opposing ideas, to understand their basis. Discuss, evaluate then either reject or assimilate. But that challenge helps to broaden our thoughts and actions and further our experiences.

You are not asked to like or enjoy all that you see, hear and feel. But, all is woven into one. It informs, it shapes and carries forward.

The different, conflicting or alternative help to refine and shape our thoughts and self. Painful questions maybe asked and hurtful self-reflection endured.

All of which is invaluable if, IF. Actions and self action arise from the bones of that dissection. Otherwise you may as well step on to the treadmill, listen to echoes and go no-where.

Do not be afraid to stand apart, to take a wider view.

As Faithless said
"Inaction is a weapon
Of mass destruction".

58

Concurrency of time and the occurrence of outcomes

There is great endeavour in working towards a goal however, be alert because it can become all encompassing. To the point where the goal is the sole focus, blinkers are worn and vision is narrowed to a pin point.

Yes this can be crucial to achieving the goal but there are traps within its path.

This moment now, what you are doing currently and that moment, that achievement to come are equally as important.

For without one the other does not exist.

Each should be treasured, for both only occur once. Even if the task is repeated it will not be the same, the anticipation, the delivery or the afterglow.

So when it is said "don't worry about now focus on the end goal". Call bullshit.

Focus on both.

The end goal will help feed the now, it will help get through the storms and encourage the riding of the momentum wave. Whilst the now funnels into the future goal, a reminder of the effort spent to get there. A reminder to enjoy that moment. Whilst knowing you have it in you to go again.

The volume does not to be turned all the way up to add value. Just because you do not rage. Does not mean you do not care.

Quiet does not mean passive. Set high standards without fanfare for beware the quiet one, while others are shouting they work on becoming what others only dare to dream about.

Appreciate the toil to reach the end goal and absorb the lessons and harvest the wisdom to apply to other aspects of your life. To share and teach others.

It is true that lofty goals often take time to come to fruition. Even more important to not lose sight of the moments along the way.

The clock is ticking and each note counts. Do not turn a blind eye to their passing in order to look to the future that is yet to arrive. For their omission carries to great a cost.

Concurrency of time and the occurrence of outcomes

If we change the view, just slightly. It is worth considering the unseen impacts of what we are doing now without even considering the possible future outcomes when we apply the timeline to life and health.

What we do now is paid forward to our older self, is a harsh a reality that too many overlook.

With cognitive dissonance too often becoming a ruling state of emotion. Putting off the future self investment for another day, for tomorrow. That becomes too easily brushed aside for the next 'tomorrow'.

Physically, mentally and emotionally the body carries its experiences forward, whether the driver of the body is aware of that or not. Happiness, trauma, activity, diet it all has its impact.

This is perhaps the greatest tightrope that we dance along. For what is the use of having a pristine body at eighty that has experienced little to nothing, a life of beige. The flip side is just as challenging. Experience everything, abuse the body and be stuck, body worn-out at fifty dependant on others.

Yes these are two extremes. I'm not suggesting one is better than the other. Only that you consider the now and the echo it creates for your future self. What's the trade-off. What do you want? What are you prepared to pay for?

DO NOT fall into the trap of thinking that 'youthfulness is wasted on the young'. Or the equally dangerous "we'll do that when we retire".

The grains of sand continue their perpetual descent through the egg timer of life. Make each one count, either now or later.

The Door

Guard your front door, chose wisely who sees what's behind it.
For the people on the outside have no idea on what is happening on the inside.

The door is exactly that.
The front of house
Then entrance to the detail behind.

Sometimes you give a glimpse.
An opportunity to see behind the door but even then it is only a mere shard of the whole picture.

We let the good bits, the happy parts be seen. The bits that convey an image, a persona that we want to have.
Sometimes that is raw and sharp, honest and blunt. For others it is carefully cultivated.

For those standing in front of the door, be mindful of all of the above.
For not everything you see is everything to be seen.
The picture shown could be a mirage, a false façade. With little substance to hold like grasping the morning mist.

There could also be the hidden pain, suffering or struggle.
Kept from the public to deal with in private and not to be
flaunted.
Battled headfirst, behind closed doors. Personally, or
with a very high-profile list of loved ones and the very
close.

Respect is required.
The very reason the bolt and spyhole exist.

If you knock
You may stay on the doorstep.

Or

You may be let in.

Either way you are always a guest.
Never the owner

Remember that.

F-E-A-R

Fear sits within all of us.

Yet we try to deny it, to bury it as if it wasn't there.

Sometimes it prickles under surface, constantly teasing us, on high alert scared of the next footstep.
Other times it waits in the deep, surrounded by shadows, shrouded in heavy silence.

For many the fear can be of rejection, failure, intimacy, success, or not being enough, of death. The fear of revealing something in us that we don't what to recognise. Perhaps all routed in the fear of not being good enough.

Certain fears are hard wired, those that are set off by immediate danger. Others are learned through experience and are often based on what might happen.

But that is normal.
It's when those fears cause paralysis the problem occurs.

Fear is not to be ignored or avoided. It's always there in different shades.
It should be recognised, met with direct eye contact. Look into it, understand where it comes from and use it.
Walk with it, by your side, do not drag it along with you.
It should not be carried, it can carry itself.

Fear is not rigid.
It is pliable.
It can be shaped and changed.

Fear is not always a negative, more often it can be an opportunity waiting to be faced. It can guide and teach, but it should never be allowed to become our master.

To Stand Apart

To be comfortable in who you are is a gift
and a rare gift at that.

For we all carry with us the burdens of
insecurities and self-doubt.
Some days they are heavy, other days they
are barely noticeable.

Created by previous cold shoulders, sharp
tongues, and the suggestion that having
different, unhomogenised goals is negative.
But there is beauty and powerful belief in
being and accepting yourself.

To stand alone, apart.
To be unalike and dissimilar to those
around you can take courage and fortitude.

Accepting that the route you are undertaking is perhaps different and potentially more challenging.
But then maybe you want a different outcome.

It does not mean that you are isolated.
There will be others heading in the same direction.
All uncommon.
A conscious choice made.

The aim is to not outshine everyone else or decry them.
More to recognise and embrace the differences whilst painting a contrasting picture.

The contrast discrete and blinding.

Resistance is to be expected.
Why do you want to do that for?
What's the point?
Only you can know the answer.

It's likely, over time, those that might have tried to dissuade you, will take notice.
Be open
Hold out a hand, maybe they want to change direction.
Maybe they have found their reason.

Just because you started alone does not mean you need to stay alone and isolated.

Maybe it is you that is wanting to reach out and take the open hand.

Understand your value. It is okay to let your light shine, it does not need to be dimmed. Do not let it be reduced by others.

Be secure.

Plant your roots.

And grow.

Sometimes it's better to stand than sit

There will always be choices to be made.
Some are clear and obvious.
Others challenging and uncomfortable.
Then there are the subtle ones, that over time have a
cumulative and significant impact. Yet in the moment
can seem insignificant.

For example: who do you sit next to?
Who do you share time and conversation with?

The person that sits next to you is more important than
you realise. They carry influence, their energy, outlook,
language, their 'vibe'.
It permeates across the space, becomes ingrained if not
checked. Remember that if you're sitting with yourself.

Time, your time is precious, once you've spent it, it
cannot be returned. Be picky with whom and how you
share it.

The time and energy involved in sharing the space, the price of that seat can become too much to bare. Yet it can also one of the greatest investments you can make.

How can you know when it's not always obvious?
Ask questions.
Be honest.
Ask more questions.

Sometimes it's better to stand than sit.
To keep moving, to stop from procrastinating or getting caught ruminating.
Movement, action, forwards.

Or to just be polite and give the seat to another. Because manners cost nothing.

Besides your hip flexors with thank you for standing.

There is always a choice

There is always a choice.

Yet frequently we are too fragile too weak to make the one we know deep down that we should.

To easily we say 'I didn't have a choice' as an excuse. Usually what it really means, deep down is we are lying to ourselves and that the easy choice was taken.

One, generally the harder one is uncomfortable and unattractive. Cloaked in thorns and fear, bringing discomfort initially but in the end leading to the result that you want. A clearer path and providing a solid foundation moving forward.

Then there is the other.

The easy choice, the path of least resistance, short and swift. Initially unlikely to cause any discomfort.

72

Yet down the line can lead to more pain, regret at having to retrace old and soiled ground. Ultimately needing to face the initial hard choice again.

Do not be swayed but external voices pulling you in the opposite direction, away from where you want to go. Standfast, hold true to yourself.

Why – that's a question only you can answer but it will require honesty.

Maybe it's due to laziness and not wanting to make the effort, because the thing you say is important actually isn't, it's just words. Actions betraying the words spoken.

Fear? Possibly but fear of what? Short sharp pain that's over quickly. Yet when avoided becomes a slow prolonged chronic and destructive issue.

Pride? Self-importance? Selfishness?

They will all play a part.

Rarely do things of value happen quickly. Shortcuts, hacks mearly prolong the inevitable. The effort needs to be made, the work done, the hard choices taken.

Take the steps.

Roll the Dice

Hardship
Struggle
Resistance
Adversity
Hurt
Set backs

At some point all likely to experience
these and more than once. Sometimes
they will be huge life changing events,
other times smaller, less significant yet
still leaving their mark.

They will in part, either be as a direct result of your own actions. In these cases ownership and learning
are crucial so repetition can be avoided. You'll be able to see the signs and stop it in its attacks be
momentum carries it away.

They can also occur through no fault or action of your own. Random things happen, randomly. Good
and bad.

While the origin or cause is not always controllable… your response is.

Seldom do you start on perfect footings if ever. In fact too much is wasted waiting for the impossibly perfect moment. We are frequently several steps back and having to catch up.

This does not mean all is lost.
It allows for a wider angle, and opportunity to build impetus and momentum. To implement the lessons of previous hardships, understanding that this too can be overcome.
The setback more of an adjustment to the course.

Life is easier with experience, but you must live to be able to gather the experience. Hiding and staying sheltered will not help. The hand you've been delt is the hand you must play.
Every roll won't be a 'Yahtzee' nor will it be 'snake eyes'. So grab the dice, roll them and play from there.

Printed in Great Britain
by Amazon